DEPRESSION
THE SILENT SHAME

by Denise L. Shaw

Adoration PRESS
Branson, Missouri

DEPRESSION – THE SILENT SHAME

Published by
ADORATION PRESS
PO Box 2253, Branson, MO 65615-2253
www.adorationpress.faithweb.com

Library of Congress Control Number: 2002094420
ISBN 0-9718685-0-6

Printed in the United States of America

DEDICATION

To Mom,
It was a price you didn't have to pay.
Thank you for being determined to persevere and overcome.

ACKNOWLEDGEMENT

To Bryan and the girls,
You bring great peace, joy and strength.
Precious gifts, I treasure all that you are.

IN LOVING MEMORY

Of Calvin & Jennifer
Your lives on this earth were valuable and important.
You are sadly missed.

CONTENTS

Chapter 1

A TENACIOUS ADVERSARY

Depression seems to have permeated every crevice of our society with more than 20% of Americans (54 million) expected to develop major depression at some point in their lifetimes.[1] Chances are, we all know someone who has been touched with this modern-day plague.

Something must be done! Wait a minute... something *has* been done.

Jesus made it clear in Luke 4:18 that He came to *"...heal the brokenhearted, to preach deliverance to the captives...to set at liberty them that are bruised"* (The Amplified Bible). There is hope and help through our Lord and Savior Jesus Christ and His anointed Word. We serve a risen Savior Who is *"...touched with the feeling of our infirmities..."* (Hebrews 4:15).

Please understand that in discussing the subject of depression, I am certainly not a medical doctor or an expert on the topic. However, due to circumstances beyond my control, I have had numerous opportunities to become *well acquainted* with this debilitating illness.

Even though I have never personally suffered from it, I have experienced first-hand its devastating effects. In my youth, I helplessly watched individual lives destroyed by something that seemed beyond their power to control – some within my own family.

1 www.webmd.com/condition center/dep, **Medical Library – Illustrated Guides, "Depression - Depression: A look Inside the Brain!"**

Out of personal tragedy and years of Bible study, the Lord has allowed me to catch a glimpse of His heart on the subject. The purpose of this book is to touch everyday people with very basic truths that will set them free from this tenacious adversary - depression.

THE SILENT SHAME

When the Lord began dealing with me to write this book, He spoke to my heart: "Depression has become the silent shame of the Church."

Over the years, research has proven if there is a problem in society as a whole, that same problem can be found (at least in a measure) within the four walls of *the Church* (divorce being a prime example).

This should not be the case. Believers in the Lord Jesus Christ are supposed to be different from the rest of the world.

We are supposed to be light in the midst of darkness, shining as bright as the noonday sun. But sadly, in many ways, especially where depression is concerned, there is little difference between believers and the rest of society.

A large percentage of those who suffer with depression are too sick, embarrassed or ashamed to seek help. Many are afraid. So, they attempt to *brush it under the rug* trying to pretend it isn't there, hoping it will just go away.

The time has come to expose this ugly thing threatening the very fiber of our society. It is time to stand up and bring some light to the issue – the Light of the World.

We can put an end to needless torment by applying the basic truths of God's Word in our daily lives. As a matter of fact, many of the principles outlined in this book will work for almost any problem we face, not just depression.

Depression or Discouragement?

Before we go any further, I want to make certain that we are *on the same page*, so-to-speak.

It is common in our society, if we're having a bad day or feeling sorry for ourselves, to tell others that we're *depressed.*

I want to make it perfectly clear that this book is not about *discouragement,* commonly referred to as *pity parties, bad moods* or *down days.* Even though those things can be helped using the same principles outlined in this book, for now we want to narrow our focus.

Primarily, we want to specifically deal with the *physiological* condition known as depression - a condition that can be diagnosed and treated by a medical professional - an illness brought on by a chemical imbalance in the body.

Depression is more than feeling sad sometimes. Medically, depression persists for more than two weeks and prevents someone from functioning in top form at work or socially. Doctors call this CLINICAL *or* MAJOR *depression.*[2]

Again, let me remind you that I am not a medical professional. However, most any physician will explain that depression can generally and simply be described as "a chemical imbalance in the brain, which

[2]"Depression," AMA Home Medical Adviser, Random House, Inc., 1988, New York.

causes nerves in the brain to not work properly," bringing about a variety of symptoms. A primary indicator of depression can be the inability to control one's thoughts - *confusion, lack of concentration, disorientation,* etc.

Other symptoms may also include one or more of the following:

- *Disruptions in sleep habits or patterns*
- *Changes in appetite*
- *Lack of pleasure in daily activities*
- *Loss of energy*
- *Recurrent headaches*
- *Feelings of worthlessness, shame or guilt*
- *Uncontrolled emotions and / or an overall feeling of melancholy*
- *Thoughts of death and / or suicide* [3 & 4]

Again, true depression is a physiological condition that can be medically diagnosed and treated. It is not *feeling sorry for oneself,* a *pity party, bad mood* or *down day.*

[3]www.webmd.com/condition center/dep, Medical Library - Illustrated Guides, "Depression- Depression: A look Inside the Brain!"

[4]"Depression," AMA Home Medical Adviser, Random House, Inc., 1988, New York.

Chapter 2

JESUS CAME TO SET US FREE

John 10:10

The thief cometh not, but for to steal, and to kill, and to destroy: I [Jesus] am come that they might have life, and that they might have it more abundantly.

Depression robs us of the abundant life Jesus came to provide.

Depression brings death and destruction in so many ways, as well as stealing our peace of mind. The ultimate source for depression is not God. The enemy of our soul seeks to destroy our very existence.

Simply knowing that depression is not from God is the first step toward freedom.

John 14:6

Jesus saith unto him, I am the way, THE TRUTH, and the life: no man cometh unto the Father, but by me.

John 8:31-32

Then said Jesus to those...which believed on him, If ye continue in my word, then are ye my disciples indeed; And ye shall know THE TRUTH, and THE TRUTH shall make you free.

Jesus said He was *the truth.* Part of His mission on earth was to present the truth that would make man free. Through His words, He gave us the keys to freedom and liberty: freedom from sin, fear, depression or whatever else may keep us from experiencing life at its best.

1 John 3:8

...For this purpose the Son of God was manifested, that he might destroy the works of the devil.

Luke 4:18-19 (The Amplified Bible)

The Spirit of the Lord [is] upon Me [Jesus], because He has anointed Me...to preach the good news (the Gospel) to the poor; He has sent Me to announce release to the captives and recovery of sight to the blind, to send forth as delivered those who are oppressed [who are downtrodden, bruised, crushed, and broken down by calamity], To proclaim the accepted and acceptable year of the Lord [the day when salvation and the free favors of God profusely abound].

What are the works of the devil?

Basically, they are anything that steals, kills or destroys. Luke 4:18-19 is God's answer concerning the works of the devil. The portion of the passage that specifically applies to depression is: *"...those who are oppressed [who are downtrodden, bruised, crushed, and broken down by calamity]..."*. Jesus came to help the depressed by *sending them forth as delivered.*

Jesus came to set us free! There is nothing too difficult for Him. There is no need so great that He cannot meet it. There is no cloud so dark that His light cannot penetrate it. He is the way, the truth, and the life. He is the ultimate source of all our help.

Grace to Help in Time of Need

Now that Jesus has ascended into heaven and is seated at the right hand of God, Hebrews 4:16 tells us that we can boldly approach God's *"...throne of grace, that we may obtain mercy, and find grace to help in time of need."* There is hope and help for those who will look to the Lord in faith.

The word *grace* has several different theological definitions. Simply put, it means *God's unmerited favor.* There is nothing we can do to earn it. Jesus already paid the price for it by shedding His innocent blood on the cross of Calvary. It is by grace we are saved.

Another definition for grace is thoroughly applicable concerning depression: *God's supernatural ability working in and through us.* It helps us deal with situations we have little or no control over - situations that seem to be out of our own realm of ability to handle.

When things seem out of control, that's when the grace of God comes to our aid to carry us up and over the storms of life.

Anytime we face circumstances beyond our own ability, we can boldly ask God for His grace and He will abundantly supply it - bringing help in our time of need.

I can't possibility count all the times I have gone to God in prayer saying, "God, your Word says I can boldly approach your throne of grace for *HELP* in time of need." He has always been faithful to supply the amount of grace needed to face the crisis at hand.

When dealing with or facing depression, it is so important to daily look to Jesus as our helper, our healer and our deliverer. He came to set us free.

Isaiah 53:3-4 (The Amplified Bible)

He was despised and rejected and forsaken by men, a Man of sorrows and pains, and acquainted with grief and sickness; and like One from Whom men hide their faces He was despised, and we did not appreciate His worth or have any esteem for Him. Surely He has borne our griefs (sicknesses, weaknesses, and distresses) and carried our sorrows and pains…

Chapter 3

POSSIBLE CAUSES

Many people fail to understand that true depression usually has some sort of cause or *trigger*. On occasion, there will seem to be no logical reason for an attack, but generally speaking, it doesn't just drop out of the sky. Most often, there are very valid reasons as to why this imbalance occurs in an individual's body.

Of course, we have already established the fact that anything that brings destruction into our lives can be ultimately attributed to our adversary – the devil. However, generally, his weapons are subtle. Very seldom do we openly see his attacks coming ahead of time.

As we discuss some of the things our enemy uses to bring this illness into the lives of the unsuspecting, let's not lose sight of the fact that Jesus came to set us free. Some of the things shared in this book could be considered *depressing*. Let us be continually reminded that there is hope and help in the Lord.

TRAUMA

One of the most surprising and devastating causes of depression can be a sudden, traumatic event. In such situations, the illness seemingly *blind-sides* an individual, bringing with it an unexpected haze of confusion and dismay.

Emotional traumas such as the death of a loved one or the dissolution of a marriage are common causes. Physical traumas such as accidents, major surgery, and childbirth can also be numbered among the more obvious triggers for depression.

Grieving can actually alter the chemical make-up of one's body. In some cases, if left alone, grief can carry a person to the point of long-term or permanent damage.

I know of a situation several years ago where a woman in my husband's family grieved so terribly over the death of her mother that she eventually lost her mind.

Even though she was a Christian, she did not know about depression or how to resist its symptoms. She refused to be comforted or to seek help. Her grief became so great she completely lost the ability to control her thinking. Thus, after numerous medical treatments, she lost nearly all of her mental faculties. She spent the remainder of her days in a nursing facility, lost in an endless haze of mental illness and confusion.

It is very common for someone who has lost a close family member to suffer with the symptoms of depression. However, for the Christian, concerning death, we must remember that 1 Thessalonians 4:13 tells us to, *"...sorrow not, even as others which have no hope."* In Christ Jesus we have the promise of eternal life. Therefore, those loved ones who *fall asleep* in the Lord have simply moved from this world into eternity. We shall see them again. There is hope.

That same Scripture passage also says, *"But I would not have you to be ignorant, brethren...."*

In my own personal life as I have experienced both the loss of a parent and grandparents, I know what it is to face grief and its side effects. Because I was not ignorant concerning these things and could recognize the early warning signs (not feeling like myself, being unusually tired and sleepy, changes in appetite, etc.), I was able to simply resist them through the Word of God.

James 4:7 instructs us to *"...Resist the devil, and he will flee..."* This Scripture is applicable in that we know from whom depression originates. Because I was able to recognize early symptoms and knew the source from which they came, I was able to resist them.

Sometimes (especially in the early stages of depression) it is simply a matter of refusing to allow the symptoms to stay in our bodies or minds – standing our ground, saying, "No, I refuse to be depressed. I choose, as an act of my will, not to sorrow as the world sorrows. I have hope. I will see that loved one again. I don't need to be discouraged. I put my hope and trust in the Lord." We must be diligent and watchful.

There is additional help available to us through the Holy Spirit. In John chapters 14 - 16, He is described as *the Comforter*. In times of grief and loss, we can look to the Lord, asking Him to send the Holy Spirit to minister comfort to our hearts and minds. It's His job.

And let's not forget about the awesome grace of God. The loss of a loved one is an opportune time to call upon Him for help in time of need (Hebrews 4:16).

Several years ago, when my father passed into eternity, it was God's grace that literally carried me through those early days. Even now it is difficult to describe the strength, comfort, and goodness of His great love that I experienced. He is faithful to answer when we call (see Psalm 4).

My first exposure to depression came at an early age. When I was eleven, my mother, brother and I were traveling on a passenger bus that was hit by a train. It was a tragic and horrific accident that took the lives of three people, as well as permanently disabling many others. Even though our injuries were minor *(Thank God for His protective Hand!)*, the physical and emotional trauma threw my mother into a depression so deep that it took years to overcome.

Of course, if we had known then what we know now, things would have been very different. As a matter of fact, it was my mother's years of suffering that caused me to seek the Lord for answers. Her story (as well as many others) was fuel for the fire - the passion in my heart to see people set free from the devastating effects of this illness.

Through the years I have watched various friends and family members struggle with depression after going through major surgery. The physical trauma of surgery commonly brings symptoms of depression. Again, let us be watchful.

Childbirth is another *biggie* where depression is concerned. It is so common it has its own term: *Baby Blues*. It is a viable challenge that many women face. As a matter of fact, I faced it after the birth of my own children. However, as with grief, I resisted it with the Word of God and that was the end of it. It left as quickly as it came.

STRESS

When depression is caused from stress, its onset is usually more subtle than with trauma. Christians shouldn't suffer in this manner if they're properly casting their cares upon the Lord. Yet, stress is a leading cause of depression (especially among the clergy). Unfortunately, it places the believer in the precarious position of sin, making the healing process a little more complicated.

First of all, a lifestyle of sin is an obvious open door for any type of attack of the enemy. Anyone purposefully engaging in sins of the flesh (see Galatians 5:16-21) is a prime target for all sorts of evil to enter into their lives, including depression.

In the life of a faithful, God-fearing believer, there are less-obvious sins that open the door to stress, which in turn can trigger depression. Pride is one of the most formidable sins. It leaves open a gaping door. Proverbs 16:18 tells us *"Pride goeth before destruction, and an haughty spirit before a fall."* It is the opposite of humility.

At its worst, pride confuses believers into thinking that they can take the position of God in their own lives, thus eliminating a need for His instruction, intervention, or wisdom. Of course, this ill-fated foolishness leads to *a fall* - resulting in failure and a lack of peace. In the end, pride-driven believers can become depressed when they discover they are not as good at doing God's job as He. Trying to do God's job for Him can be very stressful.

Two other *sins* we'll briefly mention are discouragement and not casting our cares upon the

Lord, both of which are closely related to pride (and more than likely have their roots in it).

Discouragement is an indicator of a lack of faith. Romans 14:23 tells us that *"...whatsoever is not of faith is sin"* and Hebrews 11:6 explains that *"...without faith it is impossible to please him: for he that cometh to God must believe...."* One sure *cure* for discouragement is God's Word. Romans 10:17 clearly states that *"...faith cometh by hearing, and hearing by the word of God."*

When we face circumstances beyond our control, the natural human tendency is to try to carry the load ourselves. This is where many believers fail to cast their cares upon the Lord. When circumstances stretch us to the limit we should be leaning upon the Lord, allowing His grace to carry us above or through the situation - anything less than this opens the door for the enemy.

Repentance A Necessity

In every instance of sin, repentance is a necessary step in the healing process. If we have opened the door to depression through the stress of sin (whether willful or unintentional), in order to activate the intervention of God, we must come to a place of repentance.

According to Vine's Expository Dictionary of New Testament Words the word *repentance* means *to be brought low, humbled.*[5] I have also heard it said, *to repent* means *to turn away from.*

Repentance is not just saying you're sorry and then continuing to do the same things over and over. Repentance is a decision to make a permanent change

[5] Vine's Expository Dictionary of New Testament Words, Fleming H. Revell Company, U.S.A., 1966.

for the better - turning away from the things that separate us from God.

First John 1:9 is a key for healing to begin: *"If we confess our sins, he is faithful and just to forgive us our sins, and to cleanse us from all unrighteousness."*

In discussing this matter, let it also be said, simple human nature tends to hang on to things from the past. Once sin has been confessed and forgiven, a believer (especially one suffering with depression) must then make a conscious effort to forgive himself.

Isaiah 43:25

I, even I, am he that blotteth out thy transgressions for mine own sake, and will not remember thy sins.

Philippians 3:13-14

Brethren, I count not myself to have apprehended: but this one thing I do, forgetting those things which are behind, and reaching forth unto those things which are before, I press toward the mark for the prize of the high calling of God in Christ Jesus.

Chapter 4

KNOW YOUR ENEMY

One of the basic ways to defeat a foe is to know his plan of attack in advance. The devil has no new *tricks up his sleeve*. If he's tried something before, he'll try it again. One of the best ways to prevent depression is to know how it works, exposing the enemy's efforts prior to an encounter.

As mentioned before, a primary indicator of depression can be an inability to control one's thoughts. When we lose our ability to concentrate or control our thinking, it promotes confusion.

If we were to ask a Christian suffering from depression, "Where's your faith?" he might reply, "I don't know. I feel so lost. I can't seem to feel anything anymore." He seems to be wandering in a thick haze of anxiety and perplexity. This is typical of the illness.

With an inability to concentrate, confusion opens the door for even more dramatic symptoms. If an individual can no longer control his or her thoughts, the enemy of our soul will come along with all sorts of oppressive feelings, trying to convince the sufferer they're his own. Feelings like shame, guilt, hopelessness and worthlessness come to the forefront as an individual's self-esteem becomes the center of his attack.

In severe cases, the individual may even report hearing voices. Even though some scientists would probably disagree, it is my personal belief that these voices are demonic spirits sent to torment and bewilder.

It's as if the enemy is just waiting for an opportunity to take advantage of the situation by bringing more turmoil and destruction into the life of the sufferer.

HEALING OR DELIVERANCE?

In times past, sadly, a large portion of society has ostracized individuals suffering with any type of mental illness. Well-meaning Christians have been quick to assume those with depression were guilty of some great sin, somehow spiritually defective, or worse yet, entertaining demons. This type of *isolation* and *judgmentalism* only proves to make matters worse, serving to confirm the fears and distorted perception of the sufferer.

We must make certain we are displaying the compassion and tender loving care of the Lord. If demonic things begin to manifest in an individual's life, it may simply be the enemy taking advantage of a bad situation (because the person is hindered in his ability to control his mind).

While it is true that an individual with depression may be experiencing great (spiritual) darkness - even demonic manifestations - the root of the illness is almost always physiological. We could minister *deliverance* to the point of exhaustion but unless an individual sufferer receives *healing* of the physical aspects of the illness, he will more than likely continue to be held captive.

A GENERATIONAL CURSE?

While we're on the subject of evil and really *spiritual* matters, let's address another related topic: generational curses - meaning *bearing punishment for the sins of previous generations.*

According to Ezekiel chapter 18, God did away with generational curses hundreds of years ago. No longer does God expect future generations to pay the price for the sins of their fathers.

Let's put ourselves in remembrance: Jesus paid the price for the sins of all mankind. Receiving Him as Lord and Savior completely exempts us from the eternal punishment for sin.

For unbelievers, each person will pay the price for his or her own sins – no more, no less.

It is a fact that people are more likely to suffer with depression if there is a family history of the illness.[6] As we said before; the enemy has no new *tricks up his sleeve.* If he attempts something once with success, he'll do it again and again, especially within a family. If he's gotten by with a particular kind of attack in one generation, assaults on future generations can be expected.

However, all it takes is *ONE* person knowing who he is in Christ to put the devil on the run.

For example, when our youngest daughter was born, she nearly died because the umbilical cord was wrapped tightly around her neck. Thank the Lord; she did not die because the Word of God prevailed mightily. We withstood the enemy's attack and she lived with no ill effects.

Later, I was reminded that both of my grandmothers lost baby girls to umbilical cord accidents at birth.

[6] www.webmd.con/condition center/dep, Medical Library – Illustrated Guides, "Depression - Depression: A look Inside the Brain!"

Was it coincidence? Was it a curse?

No. It was just a *washed up old devil* trying something he had successfully accomplished before in my family. Only this time it didn't work. We knew of our redemption from whatever weapon or *curse* he tried to bring our way. All we had to do was exercise our right to walk free from his plan of destruction and death.

It's Not Necessarily Anyone's Fault

Due to the nature of depression, there is usually a tremendous amount of shame and guilt associated with it. The sufferer may ask himself dozens of times: "What's wrong with me?" "How could I have let this happen?" When in actuality, he may have done nothing wrong.

God said in Hosea 4:6 that His *"...people are destroyed for lack of knowledge...."* If we don't understand something, the chances for destruction are greater. There is a tremendous amount of ignorance in our society concerning this debilitating illness.

It's important to understand how depression operates and what can cause it. Those who are familiar with it are less likely to be taken captive because they can recognize it when it comes and simply resist it.

I have a precious friend in the ministry that was completely blind-sided by a serious attack after the birth of her first child. She underwent an emergency Caesarean section and was awake for eight days straight before being hospitalized and diagnosed with manic depression (aka bi-polar disorder).

She knew nothing about the illness or how it first surfaces. Nor did she know there was a history of the illness in her family – a secret that had been kept from her throughout her childhood.

She is a strong, Spirit-filled Christian – a pastor's wife – well educated in the truths of God's Word concerning healing and the authority of the believer. Had she been a little more informed about the illness and her family's history, she might have been better prepared to face it head-on.

Once she started her recovery, she was able to practice what she preaches, ministering to herself in a very powerful way. She now has a productive life helping her husband with their church.

They went through some very rough days that could have been avoided. It wasn't her fault.

The Father of Lies

In John 8:44, Jesus said of the devil, *"...there is no truth in him. When he speaketh a lie, he speaketh of his own: for he is a liar, and the father of it."* Regardless of the circumstance, the enemy's main weapon and/or plan of attack will most assuredly contain falsehoods of some sort.

Sufferers of depression will often be bombarded in their minds with deceitful thoughts such as:

* God is punishing you or trying to teach you a lesson.
* You deserve every bad thing that happens to you. You're worthless.
* You'll never get better.
* How could you have let this happen to yourself? It's your fault.
* You'd be better off dead.

Regardless of the situation, if the enemy tells us a lie, then the opposite must be true. Jesus is the Way, *THE TRUTH* and the Life; Satan is the father of lies.

Several years ago, I went through a short phase of challenges. It seemed everywhere I turned there was some sort of trial. Because I neglected to spend enough time in the Word of God, I drifted to a place where victory seemed beyond my grasp. I began to doubt my own faith.

Then God, in His great mercy, reminded me that according to Romans 12:3, I did have faith. (Romans 12:3 states that *"...God hath dealt to every man the measure of faith."*)

I suddenly realized that I had believed a lie; a lie the enemy had been telling me in order to keep me defeated. When I recognized that fact, I understood that the opposite must be true ... I did have faith. *I DID HAVE FAITH!*

At that point, the situation turned around as I reminded the devil (and myself) of the reality of my redemption - that I was victorious through Christ (see 2 Corinthians 2:14). Within a very short period of time, I was completely free. It was that simple.

We must be watchful to make certain we are not deceived. We know the source from which lies come. Too many good people have entered into eternity prematurely because they believed a lie:

* They believed it was God's will for them to be sick. (The Word of God promises healing.)
* They believed they were going to die in some terrible accident. (The Word of God promises divine protection.)

* They believed it was their fate die young. (The Word of God promises long life.)

They received what they believed. Matthew 9:29 says, *"...According to your faith be it unto you."*

Faith plays a big part in determining our destiny.

Condemnation

What if a person has done something to open the door to depression? Romans 8:1 tells us there is no condemnation to those who are in Christ Jesus.

I have heard ministers use the prophet Elijah as an example of someone in the Bible that suffered with depression. As far as I'm concerned, there's not enough information in the 19th chapter of First Kings to determine if Elijah was truly depressed or just feeling sorry for himself. We certainly can't be dogmatic about it.

Whether Elijah suffered from depression or not, it's important to note that God's dealings with him were very gentle and supernatural. Angels attended him and he experienced a personal visitation from the Lord (see 1 Kings 19:4-12).

Acts 10:34 tells us *"...God is no respecter of persons."* That means the mercy and loving kindness available to Elijah is available to all!

Chapter 5

A TWO-FOLD BLESSING

Since persons suffering with depression are dealing with a physical condition as well as possible demonic oppression, most often they are in need of a two-fold blessing from God. They need deliverance from the enemy (oppression, fear, condemnation, etc.) as well as a need for physical healing. The good news: God has already abundantly supplied both these things through Christ's redemptive work on the cross.

The term *deliverance* in its most basic definition is *to be made free*. We have already established the fact that Jesus came to set us free. As we focus our eyes upon the victory found in Him, we will find deliverance is always based solidly in His Word.

Our Weapons

Once we start reminding the enemy (and ourselves) of who we are in Christ - that we are not our own, we've been ransomed with the precious blood of Jesus - he won't stick around. The blood of Jesus is the one weapon God used to defeat the devil.

That's right, he is a defeated foe. According to Colossians 2:15, Jesus *"...spoiled principalities and powers, he made a shew of them openly, triumphing over them in it."* That means He defeated all the powers of darkness triumphantly. The moment we are born again, we are washed in the blood of Jesus, marked and set apart, making it possible for us to say, "Can't touch this, devil."

Isaiah 54:17

No weapon that is formed against thee shall prosper...This is the heritage of the servants of the LORD, and their righteousness is of me, saith the LORD.

When we are born again, we are cleansed with the righteousness found only in the Lord Jesus Christ. Nothing the enemy tries to do to us should be successful because of the righteousness Jesus died to provide.

Some folks have a hard time believing they are righteous enough to receive anything from God. The key is remembering it is not *our* righteousness; it is the righteousness of Christ that puts us in right standing with God. Our righteousness (apart from the blood of Jesus) is as filthy rags (Isaiah 64:6).

Another weapon we have available to us (because of Christ's redemptive work) is the Name of Jesus. Jesus said in Matthew 28:18 that all power (authority) was given to Him in heaven and in earth. Philippians 2:10 says, *"That at the name of Jesus every knee should bow, of things in heaven, and things in earth, and things under the earth."*

Oftentimes, believers fail to realize that things under the earth (all spirits of darkness) are subject to the Name of Jesus. The half-brother of Jesus tells us in James 2:19 that *"...the devils also believe, and tremble...."*

If individuals suffering from depression will learn to use the Name of Jesus against oppression, those dark clouds of despair will lift the instant His Name is spoken.

I vividly remember the first time I ever used the Name of Jesus against a spiritual attack. I was a teenager living at home - hopelessly paralyzed by a fear of thunderstorms.

From my childhood I had learned to entertain *fear* by watching my parents pace from window to window the moment clouds darkened the skies. By the time I was 17, the first clap of thunder would send chills down my spine and bring heaviness upon my chest so stifling I could hardly breathe.

Second Timothy 1:7 clearly reveals that fear is a spirit. It is an evil spirit intended to rob us of our faith and our peace of mind.

My pastor at the time had been teaching a series of messages about the Name of Jesus. He had explained that if we simply speak Jesus' Name, evil spirits (including fear) have to leave us alone. I decided to give it a try.

A few days later I was awakened in the wee hours of the morning by the familiar clap of thunder. Immediately, that heavy feeling of fear gripped my throat and chest. My hands got clammy. I began to perspire. Seemingly paralyzed, I thought, "Well, here it goes..."

Through trembling lips, I whispered, "Jesus." Then, with a little more courage, "Fear, you have to go in Jesus' Name."

It fled instantly. Wow!

The next night, I didn't whisper. I boldly commanded. It left me never to return.

To this day, I thoroughly enjoy a good thunderstorm - a regular reminder of the complete victory a young girl found in the Name of Jesus.

HEALING

The second blessing needed by a sufferer of depression is healing. Even after the enemy is rendered ineffective - oppression no longer being an issue - as long as a chemical imbalance remains in the brain, there is still a problem.

It is so wonderful to know that the same Jesus Who shed His blood for our redemption; the same Jesus Who gave us His Name is the same Jesus who took stripes upon His back for our healing.

1 Peter 2:24

Who his own self [Jesus] bare our sins in his own body on the tree, that we, being dead to sins, should live unto righteousness: by whose stripes ye were healed.

Isaiah 53:4-5 (The Amplified Bible)

Surely He has borne our griefs (sicknesses, weaknesses, and distresses) and carried our sorrows and pains...and with the stripes [that wounded] Him we are healed and made whole.

Healing belongs to every believer as part of our redemptive rights.

There are many ways for a believer to receive healing from the Lord. *Step One* is to ask and believe.

Again, some folks have a hard time believing they're worthy or righteous enough to receive healing.

But, thank God, His blessings are not contingent upon *our* righteousness – they're based upon our belief on Him and *His* righteousness.

Matthew 7:7-12

Ask, and it shall be given you; seek, and ye shall find; knock, and it shall be opened unto you: For every one that asketh receiveth; and he that seeketh findeth; and to him that knocketh it shall be opened…how much more shall your Father which is in heaven give good things to them that ask him?

Healing is a *good thing.*

James 4:2

…ye have not, because ye ask not.

My first encounter with the healing power of God was during my college years. I suffered with a congenital birth defect (a tilted pelvis) that caused me to dislocate my hip on occasion. As my body matured, the instances became more frequent. By the time I reached my early twenties, it had become very annoying and painful.

At the time, I had many misconceptions about healing. I didn't think it was available to believers in our day and age. Even if it was available, I didn't think I was good enough to be healed or I thought I had to do something to earn it. Thank God, He was willing to prove me wrong.

One night, while visiting in another believer's home, I dislocated my hip. Out of God's great mercy and through the simple faith of another, He reached down His mighty hand and touched me. I was instantly healed when the gifts of the Spirit were manifested on my behalf - right there in her dining room (see Mark 16:17-18 and 1 Corinthians 12:10).

I have never dislocated my hip again. It's been nearly 20 years.

According to James 5:15, a person can call for the elders of the Church to anoint him with oil and *"...the prayer of faith will save the sick and the Lord will raise him up..."*.

An excellent example of the prayer of faith is found in Mark 11:22-24: *"And Jesus answering saith unto them, Have faith in God. For verily I say unto you, That whosoever shall say unto this mountain, Be thou removed, and be thou cast into the sea; and shall not doubt in his heart, but shall believe that those things which he saith shall come to pass; he shall have whatsoever he saith. Therefore I say unto you, What things soever ye desire, when ye pray, believe that ye receive them, and ye shall have them."*

Sometimes, if an illness (such as a cold) tries to attack my body, I will exercise faith in prayer based on Mark 11:23-24. I'll say something like this: "Mark 11:23-24 says I can have whatsoever I say and I say, 'Sickness, you can't live in my body. Jesus is my healer and He is healing me. He keeps me healthy, whole and well. According to the Word of God, my healing has been bought and paid for by the stripes Jesus took on His back. Sickness you have to go. You cannot stay in my body because Jesus is my healer. I receive my healing now according to the Word of God.'"

It doesn't take long for illness to get out of the way. It will always respond to a prayer prayed in faith.

The Work of the Holy Spirit

In discussing our weapons, we want to make sure we do not discount the work of the Holy Spirit. God is an *on-time* God. Oftentimes, He will move *suddenly* to bring healing and deliverance - as He did when He reformed my hip. We need to look no further than the four gospels to see Jesus and the goodness of God in action.

It is possible for a person to be instantly healed and delivered from depression. As a matter of fact, we've often seen it happen in services we've conducted. God is faithful to confirm His Word *"...with signs following."* (Mark 16:20).

In such instances, we still try to make sure folks understand the importance of *working* the Word of God. When individuals are healed of depression (or other mental illnesses) a firm foundation in the Scriptures must be maintained. Because of the nature of mental illness and the tenacity of our enemy, the Word of God is an important key to sustained mental health after healing is received.

Chapter 6

THE WORD IS POWERFUL

The Word of God is another weapon available to us - a weapon many believers do not learn to use effectively. Sometimes we fail to understand the magnitude of the anointing (the power of God) that is upon His Word. The inspired Scriptures have a unique touch upon them - unlike any other written work.

Second Timothy 3:16 says, *"every scripture is God-breathed (given by His inspiration)..."* (The Amplified Bible). Hebrews 4:12 tells us that *"the word of God is quick, and powerful... a discerner of the thoughts and intents of the heart."*

The Word of God, in and of itself, is so anointed that every believer can initiate deliverance for himself simply by speaking and meditating upon the Scriptures. A believer can initiate his own healing with the same principle. And, both these things, deliverance and healing, are maintained in like manner.

It is a matter of filling our hearts, minds and mouths with what the Bible says. As we speak the Word of God, reminding the enemy of his defeat and our victory in Christ (see 2 Corinthians 2:14), we put our adversary on the run, initiating our own freedom through the spoken Word.

Darkness is tenacious, but our God is greater. First John 4:4 tells us *"Greater is he that is in you, than he that is in the world."* Our enemy (the devil) is of this world but victory is on the inside of each one of us! The more of the Word of God we hide in our hearts, the more effective we will be in using it as a weapon against every foe that comes our way.

Proverbs 4:20-22

My son, attend to my words; incline thine ear unto my sayings. Let them not depart from thine eyes; keep them in the midst of thine heart. For they are life unto those that find them, and health to all their flesh.

The same Word of God that brings deliverance from our enemy also brings health to our flesh. Dozens of promises for the healing of our physical bodies can be found throughout the Scriptures. Once the devil has been dealt with, the same principle - speaking and meditating upon the Word of God - can be used for healing our bodies - even the most severe forms of mental illness.

I know of a man who was diagnosed several years ago with paranoid schizophrenia (a term doctors sometimes use to describe a medical condition in the brain that causes severe mental instability). Sufferers are known to have extremely bizarre behavior and often report hallucinations and hearing voices. This gentleman was one such individual.

The one thing this man had going for him was the fact that he was born again *and* he believed that God could heal him. His only hope of recovery was in the Lord since there was no medical cure for his condition.

Of course, people thought he was crazy (and, assuredly, he was). So, what did he have to loose?

He went to his pastor and explained his desire to receive healing. He received solid instruction from the

Word of God. He learned how to use his weapons and his pastor helped him discover Scriptures that really ministered to his heart and spoke healing to his body.

On a *good* day, he recorded himself speaking the Scriptures they had found. He would speak each passage to himself over and over again - day in and day out - 30, 60, up to 100 times a day. He had been wisely counseled to ignore the voices he heard to the best of his ability and simply speak the Word. So, on *bad* days, when the voices were the worst, he played the recording of himself speaking the Word over and over.

This man, basically, initiated his own deliverance and healing simply by speaking and meditating upon the Word of God. He proclaimed his healing nearly two years before doctors took notice. (They thought he was crazy.) He eventually received a clean bill of health and was released from all medications and medical attention.

On the flip side of this glorious story, there is tragedy. For every victory, there are countless others who never hear about or understand the value of God's Word.

Many years ago, we had a dear family member diagnosed with major depression. He was hospitalized on more than one occasion for treatment. To me, the most tragic portion of his story is the fact that upon entry into a mental health facility, the doctors forbid him to have a Bible, citing it as a source of confusion to the patient.

We must understand that according to 1 Corinthians 14:33, *"God is not the author of confusion, but of peace..."*.

Most assuredly, God is the inspiration behind the Scriptures. Rightly divided, the Word of God is the ONE thing that can truly alleviate confusion and bring peace.

Some folks get confused because the enemy will try to twist Scripture into saying something it does not mean.

In the gospel accounts of Jesus' temptation, the devil tried to use Scripture as one of his tools of deception. Jesus didn't lie down and let the devil have the upper hand. No. He spoke the Word of God back to him by saying "It is written," completely thwarting the enemy's attack.

The Word of God is not the source of confusion. Confusion comes directly from the enemy of our soul. If confusion is present, we can know that God is not behind it. He is not the author of confusion.

If my loved one could have properly applied the Word of God, it would have been the one thing to bring lasting and total recovery.

Without the Word of God, he was without hope.

He took his own life at the age of 24, leaving a young wife and two small children. He thought his family would be better off without him.

He believed a lie.

WHY SPEAK THE WORD?

Joshua 1:8

This book of the law SHALL NOT DEPART OUT OF THY MOUTH; but thou shalt MEDITATE therein day and night, that thou mayest observe to do according to all that is written therein: for then thou shalt make thy way prosperous, and then thou shalt have good success.

Speaking what we believe is such an important spiritual truth. In most instances, it means the difference between victory and defeat.

In the book of beginnings, Genesis, we see that God spoke *creation* into existence. He then made man in His image. The account of man's creation in the original Hebrew language indicates that man is a *speaking* spirit. We are the only creatures on earth with this ability.

God intended for man to be able to speak as He speaks. Just as God created the heavens and the earth with His Word, so we form our *worlds* - the circumstances around us - with the words we speak.

The Scripture passage we referred to previously concerning the prayer of faith, Mark 11:23-24, actually references *speaking* or *saying* four times, reaffirming the truth that *we have what we say.*

In Romans 4:17 the Apostle Paul explains that Abraham called *"...those things which be not as though they were."* In other words, regardless of what Abraham saw or the circumstances that surrounded him, he said what he believed. He spoke as if his words had already occurred - and eventually they came to pass.

Jesus used this same principle in raising Jairus' daughter from the dead. Even though she had been pronounced dead and the mourners were already there to comfort the family, Jesus said in Luke 8:52, *"...Weep not; she is not dead, but sleepeth."* He spoke those things that were not as though they were. He then raised her from the dead.

We can apply this principle concerning our mental health and stability. We may be confused or bewildered, but if we say what God says about us (such as "I have the mind of Christ" or "I have a sound mind"), eventually those things will line up with what we say.

Meditate means *to mutter to oneself* (under one's breath), which indicates there is more to it than simply *thinking*. The absolute best way to control our thoughts is by *saying* with our mouths. If we will speak God's Word (muttering to ourselves) we can override wrong thoughts with the truth.

Chapter 7

JOY AND THE SPIRIT-FILLED LIFE

Nehemiah 8:10

...the joy of the LORD is your strength.

Psalm 28:7

The LORD is my strength and my shield; my heart trusted in him, and I am helped: therefore my heart greatly rejoiceth; and with my song will I praise him.

Rejoicing and joy are necessary keys to walking free and staying free. The nature of depression is to amble about in a cloud of melancholy and gloom. Rejoicing and joy drive away such things in a whisper.

In reality, rejoicing is most often something we do by choice. We cannot live our lives according to how we feel. If we live by how we feel, many of us would never get out of bed in the mornings. Our lives are made up of the choices we make. There are days when we all need to choose joy.

I remember, in the early years of our marriage (when money was *tight*), getting up once in the middle of the night worrying over bills. At the time, I was just a few weeks from giving birth to our first child - and extremely *hormonal*. I waddled the floor, stewed and fretted, fretted and stewed and then waddled some more.

Quite unexpectedly, I found myself thinking, "This is ridiculous. God has always taken care of us. There's not really anything I can do. I'm not really helping by fretting. I'm just going to take a moment and praise the Lord to show Him that I trust Him."

By this time, I was sobbing. So, in the most pitiful voice imaginable, I bawled through a red face (streaked with tears), "I praaaaise You, God. (Sniff, sniff) I looooove You, Jesus. I magnify Yoooooou. I maggggnify You. I magnify You?"

Suddenly, I found myself trying to picture what it would be like to look at God through a magnifying glass. You know, He's a pretty big God. But when we put Him under a magnifying glass, He gets REALLY BIG. The longer I "magnified" Him, the bigger He got. By the time I came to myself, my problems seemed like teeny tiny specks compared to Him and the greatness of His love.

When I started, I didn't *feel* like praising Him. I wanted to crawl under a rock somewhere and have a huge *pity party*. Praising Him was a choice I made. Because of that choice, He blessed me. The joy of the Lord truly became my strength. Then I got happy. I found myself *rejoicing* all over the living room.

I went back to bed and slept in sweet peace. I never fussed about that situation again. Our finances didn't turn around instantly - it took some time - but we didn't go under either. His joy sustained me because I chose to praise Him in that hour of darkness.

Proverbs 17:22

A merry heart doeth good like a medicine...

There have been many studies that have proven laughter is the best medicine - something the Word of God has been saying for thousands of years. I recently heard of a report that indicates laughter actually releases healing chemicals in the brain - a definite plus for individuals enduring the agony of depression.

Praise is an excellent companion to joy and laughter. It is often the catalyst that helps us *break forth into joy*. Psalm 22:3 tells us that God inhabits the praises of His people. When we praise Him, He shows up. There is nothing like experiencing His manifested presence. Gloom and despair melt like wax in the presence of the Lord.

Praise and thanksgiving are outstanding ways to express what's in our hearts. The enemy will not hang around when we praise God.

Praise and thanksgiving are awesome ways to exercise or demonstrate our faith.

It's not always easy to praise the Lord, especially when we don't feel like it.

It pleases the Lord when we put our feelings aside and thank Him in advance. Plus, it keeps our minds occupied, keeping them from wandering into the shadows of desolation.

Ephesians 5:18-20

...be filled with the Spirit; Speaking to yourselves in psalms and hymns and spiritual songs, singing and making melody in your heart to the Lord; Giving thanks always for all things unto God and the Father in the name of our Lord Jesus Christ.

Maintaining a spirit-filled life is an important factor. The aforementioned example about magnifying God is also a good illustration of Ephesians 5:18-20. I spoke to myself. I sang and praised Him. I gave Him thanks.

Because I praised and thanked Him, He filled me up. When I poured my heart out to Him, He poured Himself into me. It was a blessing that sustained me through very difficult times.

If joy and laughter seem out of the realm of possibility, we should praise the Lord. Eventually, we will find God has poured Himself into us and filled us with His goodness. Then joy and laughter will come, helping us to remember what it feels like to be happy again.

Chapter 8

DON'T BEAR THE BURDEN ALONE

Hebrews 13:5

...for he[Jesus] hath said, I will never leave thee, nor forsake thee.

Matthew 18:20

For where two or three are gathered together in my name, there am I in the midst of them.

Isolation is one of the most dangerous symptoms of depression. Usually because of shame or fear, sufferers often cut themselves off from everything and everyone - especially from those who can help the most.

Not long ago, I lost a dear friend because of this illness. She did not understand how depression attacks. Perhaps she thought since she was a Bible-school graduate she could handle it on her own. She was ashamed and confused. Only her closest family members knew, and they were not qualified to help her. They lived in fear instead of seeking outside help. Even her closest friends and pastors did not know what she was going through until it was too late. It was her death that finally moved me to write this book.

If you know (or even suspect) others may be going through depression, do not abandon them to handle it on their own. Reach out to them or find someone who will. It is vitally important for sufferers of depression to receive help from someone who can be trusted, someone who is patient and kind, one who is well acquainted with the Word of God.

Self-help should never be our only option.

When dealing with depression, a person has a tendency to get confused and disoriented. Regular church attendance and a good pastor can be important keys to victory. Fellowshipping with strong, spirit-filled believers provides support and encouragement not found elsewhere.

I mentioned in a previous chapter that my mother had suffered with depression for several years as a result of trauma. In my adolescence, it was difficult for me to understand why she seemed to be *worse* on Sunday mornings than any other time during the week.

As I matured and learned of the enemy's tactics, it became obvious to me how the devil would attack. Her worst days would cause her to isolate herself, keeping her from being exposed to the very things that would bring the most comfort and help.

The enemy knows the value of assembling together with other believers (see Hebrews 10:25). It's amazing how many in the Body of Christ fail to see the validity of this truth. We need to recognize his deception and start putting what we know into practice.

Remember, a banana away from the bunch gets peeled. Let's go to church.

Chapter 9

MEDICAL ASSISTANCE AND WISDOM

Proverbs 4:7

Wisdom is the principal thing; therefore get wisdom: and with all thy getting get understanding.

James 5:5

If any of you lack wisdom, let him ask of God...and it shall be given him.

Medical assistance and medication is a big issue. Just because this book focuses on the *spiritual* aspects of walking free from depression does not mean that I am against medical science. As a matter of fact, I believe wholeheartedly that God is the author of most medical advances and breakthroughs. Were it not for medical science, there would be a lot fewer Christians alive and well today.

Every situation is different and, medically speaking, must be handled on an individual basis. What works for one person may not work for another. Some individuals can't gain enough control of their minds to even put together a complete thought, let alone speak and meditate upon the Word of God. In these cases, a person may need to seek medical assistance. Medication can often help an individual regain enough of his mental faculties to get on top of the situation.

If possible, it would be wise to find a good doctor who is willing to work with the individual's faith. In *some* cases, it is possible to gradually phase out medication as healing is manifested in the body - but I must stress the importance of allowing a medical professional to regulate the dosage of prescription drugs. Sadly, some men and women of *faith* stopped taking proper medication before their bodies were completely healed, ending up in a mess.

For some, there are also dietary issues. Vitamin deficiencies or food allergies can sometimes contribute to the severity of an imbalance. Diets high in carbohydrates have also been known to have an effect on mental stability. It might be wise to contact a local nutritionist for assistance in this area.

Chapter 10

NO JESUS, NO PEACE – KNOW JESUS, KNOW PEACE

The word *peace* in the original Hebrew is *Shalom*. Simply defined *shalom* means *the peace that comes from being whole* - *whole* meaning *nothing missing, nothing broken*.

It is not possible to know true peace without knowing the Prince of Peace, Jesus Christ. When we enter into a relationship with the Lord, we find what it truly means to know peace.

Often Christianity is confused with other religions of the world. But, in reality, Christianity is not about *religion* - it's about *relationship*. A relationship with the Lord Jesus Christ brings peace that passes all understanding - a very important key in overcoming depression and staying free.

I would be remiss as a believer of the gospel (the good news) if I didn't offer our readers an opportunity to know this blessed Savior Who makes us whole.

Perhaps some of you have never known the peace that comes from being whole; the peace that comes from knowing Him. This chapter is designed for you.

Perhaps some readers already know Him as Lord, but have strayed in their relationship with Him. Let's not drift so far from Him that we cease to intimately experience His wonderful ways.

It's not difficult to enter into a relationship with the Savior. Romans 10:9-10 says, *"That if thou shalt confess with thy mouth the Lord Jesus, and shalt believe in thine heart that God hath raised him from the dead, thou shalt be saved. For with the heart man believeth unto righteousness; and with the mouth confession is made unto salvation."* It's that simple.

Let's pray this prayer aloud:

Dear Heavenly Father, I come to you in the Name of Jesus. I believe He is your Son, that He died on the cross for my sins, that You raised Him from the dead, and that He is now seated at Your right hand. Because I believe, I confess Jesus as my Lord and Savior. I know that as I receive Him as my Lord, I receive forgiveness for all my sins. According to Your Word, as I believe and confess, I am saved. Thank You Lord, for saving me and cleansing me with the precious Blood of Jesus. Thank You, Lord for loving me unconditionally. I receive Your love and purpose in my heart to live for You. In Jesus' Name, Amen.

SCRIPTURES FOR INSPIRATION, MEDITATION AND CONFESSION

For the convenience of the reader, I have selected a number of Scripture passages that will be helpful in getting started with speaking and meditating upon the Word of God.

I encourage you to refer to these Scriptures often. Read them. Write them. Memorize them.

Many of the selections are not just about God – they are about you and who you are in Him. *Speak* them. *Believe them!*

They will bring *light* where there has been darkness, *hope* where there has been discouragement, and *peace* where there has been confusion and dismay.

May the Lord bless and keep you as you give His Word first place in your life.

John 8:31-32

Then said Jesus to those…which believed on him, If ye continue in my word, then are ye my disciples indeed; And ye shall know THE TRUTH, *and* THE TRUTH *shall make you free.*

John 8:36

If the Son therefore shall make you free, ye shall be free indeed.

Luke 4:18-19 (The Amplified Bible)

The Spirit of the Lord [is] upon Me [Jesus], because He has anointed Me…to preach the good news (the Gospel) to the poor; He has sent Me to announce release to the captives and recovery of sight to the blind, to send forth as delivered those who are oppressed [who are downtrodden, bruised, crushed, and broken down by calamity], To proclaim the accepted and acceptable year of the Lord [the day when salvation and the free favors of God profusely abound].

John 10:10

The thief cometh not, but for to steal, and to kill, and to destroy: I am come that they might have life, and that they might have it more abundantly.

John 14:6

Jesus saith unto him, I am the way, THE TRUTH, *and the life: no man cometh unto the Father, but by me.*

2 Timothy 1:7

For God hath not given us the spirit of fear; but of power, and of love, and of a sound mind.

1 Corinthians 2:16

… But we have the mind of Christ.

Philippians 2:5

Let this mind be in you, which was also in Christ Jesus.

Romans 8:37

No, in all these things we are more than conquerors through him who loved us.

1 Corinthians 15:57

But thanks be to God! He gives us the victory through our Lord Jesus Christ.

2 Corinthians 2:14

Now thanks be unto God, which always causeth us to triumph in Christ, and maketh manifest the savour of his knowledge by us in every place.

Isaiah 54:17

No weapon that is formed against thee shall prosper…This is the heritage of the servants of the LORD, and their righteousness is of me, saith the LORD.

1 John 4:4

Ye are of God, little children, and have overcome them: because greater is he that is in you, than he that is in the world.

James 4:7

Submit yourselves therefore to God. Resist the devil, and he will flee from you.

1 John 3:8

…For this purpose the Son of God was manifested, that he might destroy the works of the devil.

Matthew 28:18

And Jesus came and spake unto them, saying, All power is given unto me in heaven and in earth.

Luke 10:19

Behold, I give unto you power to tread on serpents and scorpions, and over all the power of the enemy: and nothing shall by any means hurt you.

Ephesians 6:12

For we wrestle not against flesh and blood, but against principalities, against powers, against the rulers of the darkness of this world, against spiritual wickedness in high places.

Philippians 2:10

That at the name of Jesus every knee should bow, of things in heaven, and things in earth, and things under the earth.

Colossians 2:15

And having spoiled principalities and powers, he made a shew of them openly, triumphing over them in it.

1 Peter 5:8-9

Be sober, be vigilant; because your adversary the devil, as a roaring lion, walketh about, seeking whom he may devour: Whom resist stedfast in the faith…

Romans 8:1-2

There is therefore now no condemnation to them which are in Christ Jesus, who walk not after the flesh, but after the Spirit. For the law of the Spirit of life in Christ Jesus hath made me free from the law of sin and death.

Philippians 3:13-14

Brethren, I count not myself to have apprehended: but this one thing I do, forgetting those things which are behind, and reaching forth unto those things which are before, I press toward the mark for the prize of the high calling of God in Christ Jesus.

1 John 1:9

If we confess our sins, he is faithful and just to forgive us our sins, and to cleanse us from all unrighteousness.

Isaiah 43:25

I, even I, am he that blotteth out thy transgressions for mine own sake, and will not remember thy sins.

Romans 10:9-10

That if thou shalt confess with thy mouth the Lord Jesus, and shalt believe in thine heart that God hath raised him from the dead, thou shalt be saved. For with the heart man believeth unto righteousness; and with the mouth confession is made unto salvation.

Matthew 7:7-12

Ask, and it shall be given you; seek, and ye shall find; knock, and it shall be opened unto you: For every one that asketh receiveth; and he that seeketh findeth; and to him that knocketh it shall be opened…how much more shall your Father which is in heaven give good things to them that ask him?

James 4:2

…ye have not, because ye ask not.

Acts 10:34

…God is no respecter of persons.

Romans 2:11

For there is no respect of persons with God.

Matthew 9:29

…According to your faith be it unto you.

Romans 10:17

...So then faith cometh by hearing, and hearing by the word of God.

Mark 11:22-24

And Jesus answering saith unto them, Have faith in God. For verily I say unto you, That whosoever shall say unto this mountain, Be thou removed, and be thou cast into the sea; and shall not doubt in his heart, but shall believe that those things which he saith shall come to pass; he shall have whatsoever he saith. Therefore I say unto you, What things soever ye desire, when ye pray, believe that ye receive them, and ye shall have them.

Romans 12:3

...God hath dealt to every man the measure of faith.

Romans 14:23

...for whatsoever is not of faith is sin.

Hebrews 11:6

But without faith it is impossible to please him: for he that cometh to God must believe that he is, and that he is a rewarder of them that diligently seek him.

Hebrews 4:12

For the word of God is quick, and powerful, and sharper than any twoedged sword, piercing even to the dividing asunder of soul and spirit, and of the joints and marrow, and is a discerner of the thoughts and intents of the heart.

Romans 12:1-2

I beseech you therefore, brethren, by the mercies of God, that ye present your bodies a living sacrifice, holy, acceptable unto God, which is your reasonable service. And be not conformed to this world: but be ye transformed by the renewing of your mind, that ye may prove what is that good, and acceptable, and perfect, will of God.

2 Timothy 3:16 (The Amplified Bible)

Every Scripture is God-breathed (given by His inspiration) and profitable for instruction, for reproof and conviction of sin, for correction of error and discipline in obedience, [and] for training in righteousness (in holy living, in conformity to God's will in thought, purpose, and action).

Joshua 1:8

This book of the law SHALL NOT DEPART OUT OF THY MOUTH; *but thou shalt* MEDITATE *therein day and night, that thou mayest observe to do according to all that is written therein: for then thou shalt make thy way prosperous, and then thou shalt have good success.*

James 1:25

But whoso looketh into the perfect law of liberty, and continueth therein, he being not a forgetful hearer, but a doer of the work, this man shall be blessed in his deed.

Proverbs 4:7

Wisdom is the principal thing; therefore get wisdom: and with all thy getting get understanding.

Proverbs 4:20-22

My son, attend to my words; incline thine ear unto my sayings. Let them not depart from thine eyes; keep them in the midst of thine heart. For they are life unto those that find them, and health to all their flesh.

Matthew 8:17

That it might be fulfilled which was spoken by Esaias the prophet, saying, Himself [Jesus] took our infirmities, and bare our sicknesses.

Isaiah 53:4-5 (The Amplified Bible)

Surely He has borne our griefs (sicknesses, weaknesses, and distresses) and carried our sorrows and pains…But He was wounded for our transgressions, He was bruised for our guilt and iniquities; the chastisement [needful to obtain] peace and well-being for us was upon Him, and with the stripes [that wounded] Him we are healed and made whole.

1 Peter 2:24

Who his own self [Jesus] bare our sins in his own body on the tree, that we, being dead to sins, should live unto righteousness: by whose stripes ye were healed.

Psalm 107:20

He sent his word, and healed them, and delivered them from their destructions.

Acts 10:38

How God anointed Jesus of Nazareth with the Holy Ghost and with power: who went about doing good, and healing all that were oppressed of the devil; for God was with him.

Hebrews 13:8

Jesus Christ the same yesterday, and to day, and for ever.

Mark 16:17-18

And these signs shall follow them that believe; In my name shall they cast out devils...they shall lay hands on the sick, and they shall recover.

1 Corinthians 12:1-10

Now concerning spiritual gifts, brethren, I would not have you ignorant...For to one is given by the Spirit... the gifts of healings...

James 5:14-15

Is any sick among you? let him call for the elders of the church; and let them pray over him, anointing him with oil in the name of the Lord: And the prayer of faith shall save the sick, and the Lord shall raise him up; and if he have committed sins, they shall be forgiven him.

2 Corinthians 3:17-18

Now the Lord is that Spirit: and where the Spirit of the Lord is, there is liberty. But we all, with open face beholding as in a glass the glory of the Lord, are changed into the same image from glory to glory, even as by the Spirit of the Lord.

Galatians 5:13

For, brethren, ye have been called unto liberty.

Ephesians 1:3

Blessed be the God and Father of our Lord Jesus Christ, who hath blessed us with all spiritual blessings in heavenly places in Christ.

Ephesians 5:18-20

...be (being) filled with the Spirit; Speaking to

yourselves in psalms and hymns and spiritual songs, singing and making melody in your heart to the Lord; Giving thanks always for all things unto God and the Father in the name of our Lord Jesus Christ.

Nehemiah 8:10

...the joy of the LORD is your strength.

Psalm 28:7

The LORD is my strength and my shield; my heart trusted in him, and I am helped: therefore my heart greatly rejoiceth; and with my song will I praise him.

Proverbs 17:22

A merry heart doeth good like a medicine...

Proverbs 18:14 (The Amplified Bible)

The strong spirit of a man sustains him in... trouble...

Hebrews 4:15-16

For we have not an high priest which cannot be touched with the feeling of our infirmities; but was in all points tempted like as we are, yet without sin. Let us therefore come boldly unto the throne of grace, that we may obtain mercy, and find grace to help in time of need.

2 Corinthians 6:14

Be ye not unequally yoked together with unbelievers: for what fellowship hath righteousness with unrighteousness? and what communion hath light with darkness?

Hebrews 10:25

Not forsaking the assembling of ourselves together, as the manner of some is; but exhorting one another: and so much the more, as ye see the day approaching.

Psalm 4

Hear me when I call, O God of my righteousness: thou hast enlarged me when I was in distress; have mercy upon me, and hear my prayer…Thou hast put gladness in my heart…I will both lay me down in peace, and sleep: for thou, LORD, only makest me dwell in safety.

Psalm 31:19

How great is your goodness, which you have stored up for those who fear you, which you bestow in the sight of men on those who take refuge in you.

ABOUT THE AUTHOR

Denise L. Shaw is a traveling minister and writer, as well as being a devoted wife and mother. She and her husband, Bryan, have a dynamic healing ministry, with special emphases on prayer and deliverance (through the Word of God). She is ordained through the Association of Faith Churches and Ministers based in Branson, Missouri and is a licensed minister with World Harvesters Ministers Network in South Bend, Indiana.

The Shaws are the founders of Adoration Ministries, Inc. In addition to evangelistic ministry, they distribute a bi-monthly publication entitled, "The Voice of Thanksgiving."

Denise was a young girl when she gave her heart to the Lord. From her childhood she has had a deep hunger and respect for the Word of God.

When she was seventeen, God confirmed His call upon her life to sing gospel music. After completing her college education, she entered one of the nation's leading Bible schools.

Since graduating from Rhema Bible Training Center in 1987, Mrs. Shaw has been actively involved in numerous aspects of ministry. She received the call to be an evangelist in April of 1994.

For information pertaining to The Shaws' itinerary, to schedule Denise as a vocalist or a speaker, or to receive a free subscription to "The Voice of Thanksgiving," requests and inquiries may be made to:

Adoration Ministries, Inc.
PO Box 2253
Branson, MO 65615-2253
www.adoration.faithweb.com

RECOMMENDED READING

The Believer's Authority and The Triumphant Church by Kenneth E. Hagin, Faith Library Publications, PO Box 50126, Tulsa, OK 74150-0126.

God's Irresistible Word and Healing: Forever Settled by Kenneth Hagin, Jr., Faith Library Publications.

The Blood and the Glory by Billye Brim, Harrison House Publishing, Tulsa, Oklahoma.